CONTENTS

Introduction — 2

Chapter 1: The Big Picture: What Is Macroeconomics? — 4

Chapter 2: Macroeconomics in Society — 8

Chapter 3: GDP and Economic Growth — 12

Chapter 4: The Balancing Act: Inflation and Deflation — 17

Chapter 5: The Government's Wallet: Fiscal Policy — 22

Chapter 6: The Central Bank's Toolkit: Monetary Policy — 26

Chapter 7: International Trade and Economics — 30

Chapter 8: Economic Cycles and Indicators — 34

Chapter 9: Macroeconomics in Action — 39

What Now? — 45

Glossary — 48

INTRODUCTION

<u>WHAT EVEN IS THIS BOOK?</u>

Given you bought this book, you are probably curious about how countries manage their money, what affects the job market, or why the cost of living goes up and down. This book is your doorway into understanding the big economic forces that shape our lives, communities, and the world.

Macroeconomics is all about the 'big picture' of economics. It's not just about individual choices or single businesses; it's about how entire countries work economically. This book will take you on a journey, with no prior knowledge needed, through different aspects of macroeconomics, such as how much stuff (like cars, food, and services) a country produces (that's called **GDP**), what happens when not enough people can find jobs (unemployment), and why sometimes things get more expensive (**inflation**).

But why should you care? Because these big economic ideas affect everything from the price of your favorite snack to whether your parents can find good jobs, and even to how much your family pays for a home. Plus, understanding economics can help you make sense of the news, make better financial decisions in the future, and even debate economic policies more confidently.

You're about to look into how the world's money moves, why it matters, and what you can do to be a part of it all. Whether you're thinking about your future career, want to be more informed about the world, or just need to ace your next economics test, this book has got you covered. Get ready to see the world in a whole new way!

CHAPTER 1

<u>THE BIG PICTURE: WHAT IS MACROECONOMICS?</u>

Welcome to economics! Imagine economics as a big, bustling city. In this city, every decision, from a single person choosing what to buy for lunch to an entire government planning its annual budget, plays an important role in how the city operates. But how do we begin to understand all these complex interactions and decisions? This is where the fields of microeconomics and macroeconomics come in. Before looking at macroeconomics, let's get an understanding of what microeconomics is.

Microeconomics: The Individual and The Market

Microeconomics is like looking at the city through a magnifying glass. It focuses on the small-scale interactions and decisions made by individuals and businesses. Think about when you decide to save your allowance to buy a new game or choose between buying a hamburger or a slice of pizza.

These decisions might seem personal and insignificant, but when millions of people make these choices every day, it shapes the economy in big ways.

Microeconomics also explores how businesses decide what to sell, how much to charge, and how many people to hire. It looks at supply and demand, the forces that drive the prices of goods and services. For example, if a new, exciting video game is released but there aren't many copies available, the price might be very high because the demand for the game is greater than the supply. Note, that some companies might artificially lower supply to get people to buy things for higher prices!

Macroeconomics: The Big Picture

Now, let's zoom out and look at the entire city from above. This is the perspective of macroeconomics. Macroeconomics is about the big picture. It examines the overall performance and structure of the economy, dealing with national and global economic trends. This includes studying things like the total goods and services produced by a country, called **GDP**, rates of unemployment, **inflation**, and how money flows between different countries.

Think about the government cutting taxes so people have more money to buy things, or a big bank changing **interest rates** to keep prices from going too high. These big choices touch everyone's lives, shaping the economy. Macroeconomics is like the tool that helps us see how the economy is doing, guess what might happen next, and make plans to help it do better.

The Connection Between Micro and Macro

While micro and macroeconomics may seem different, they are deeply connected. The choices made by individuals and businesses (the micro level) add up to shape the larger economic trends (the macro level). For instance, if many companies decide to hire more workers, this can reduce the overall **unemployment rate**, a macroeconomic indicator.

Similarly, decisions made at the macro level affect the micro level. If the government increases taxes on businesses, this could lead to higher prices for products and services, affecting individual spending choices and business decisions, in turn affecting the micro.

Why Both Perspectives Are Important

Learning about both small-scale (micro) and large-scale (macro) economics helps us understand how the economy works. This understanding helps everyone, from working citizens to business owners and those making laws, to make better choices. It allows us to make sense of news, see how government decisions impact us, and get why certain big events happen in the world.

Here is an example; in a small city, Mrs. Lee runs a popular bakery, focusing on how she decides what breads to bake and at what prices to sell them. Meanwhile, the city decides to improve the roads and parks nearby, a macroeconomic action to enhance the community's overall well-being and economic health. These improvements attract more visitors, increasing Mrs. Lee's sales. Microeconomic decisions made within a business and macroeconomic policies made in the city complement each other.

CHAPTER 2
MACROECONOMICS IN SOCIETY

Now let's go a bit deeper into macro territory. Macroeconomics isn't just something you learn in school; it's a useful way to look at the world. It helps us understand why events happen that affect our lives, our communities, and the whole world.

Guiding Government Policy

A key job of macroeconomics is to help guide what the government does in terms of policymaking. Governments have the challenging task of making decisions that affect the economic well-being of their citizens. Through macroeconomic analysis (studying indicators that you will learn about later in this book), policymakers can understand the current state of the economy and predict future trends. This knowledge enables them to craft policies that aim to stabilize the economy, reduce unemployment, control **inflation**, and encourage economic growth.

For example, when the economy is doing poorly, governments might roll out **stimulus packages** to kickstart spending and investment. Macroeconomic theories guide how big these packages should be and what they should include to make sure they help and don't cause problems.

Shaping Monetary Policy

Monetary policy is actions which are taken to control a nation's money supply. Central banks, like the Federal Reserve in the United States or the European Central Bank in Europe, look at macroeconomic indicators to guide their **monetary policy**. This includes setting **interest rates** and controlling the money supply. These actions can cool down an overheated economy (one that has a long period of growth, and lots of money changing hands) or stimulate a sluggish one.

For example, if **inflation** is high, a central bank might increase **interest rates** to reduce spending and borrowing, which can help bring **inflation** down. Central banks use macroeconomic data and analysis to make decisions that help keep prices stable and support economic growth.

Influencing Business Decisions

Businesses operate in a broader economic environment that influences their operations, growth, and profitability. Macroeconomic trends such as consumer spending, economic growth rates, and **inflation** can have significant impacts on businesses. Companies use macroeconomic analysis to make informed decisions about investment, expansion, hiring, and inventory management.

For example, if macroeconomic indicators suggest an upcoming recession, businesses might tighten their budgets, delay expansion plans, or focus on cost-cutting measures to weather the economic downturn.

Impacting Individual Lives

While macroeconomics deals with the economy at a large scale, its effects are deeply personal. Economic policies and conditions influence our employment opportunities, wages, prices of goods and services, and overall quality of life. If we understand macroeconomics, it can help individuals make better financial decisions, such investing or retirement.

Also, in a democratic society, informed citizens can participate more effectively in public debate and advocate for policies that promote economic stability and growth.

Fostering Global Understanding and Cooperation

In our interconnected world, the economic fate of nations is closely linked. By analyzing global economic trends, countries can coordinate policies with each other to manage global challenges such as financial crises, climate change, and poverty.

The role of macroeconomics in society is profound and pervasive. It guides policymakers, influences business strategies, impacts individual financial decisions, and fosters international cooperation.

CHAPTER 3
<u>GDP AND ECONOMIC GROWTH</u>

What is GDP and Why Does it Matter?

Gross Domestic Product, or **GDP**, is like the scoreboard of a country's economy. It measures the total value of all goods and services produced over a specific time period within a nation's borders. Imagine adding up the money from everything—from the number of cars and smartphones manufactured to the haircuts given and movies made. The total gives us the **GDP**.

But why does this massive number matter? **GDP** is a key indicator of a country's economic health. A growing **GDP** means the economy is flourishing: businesses are producing more, people are finding jobs, and living standards are improving. Conversely, if **GDP** is shrinking, it could signal trouble, such as rising unemployment and lower spending power among citizens.

Understanding Economic Growth

Economic growth occurs when a country's **GDP** increases over time. It's like watching a plant grow; just as a plant needs water and sunlight, the economy needs investment and consumption to expand. Economic growth is driven by various factors, including technological advancements, increases in workforce size and quality, and investments in infrastructure.

India's GDP in 2023 was $3.7 trillion, while California's GDP was $3.9 trillion. Now how is it that the GDP of California with only 39 million people was able to surpass the GDP of India with 1.4 billion people? (35x times the size of California's!) Any guesses? Turns out the investments the United States has made over the years into technology and innovation have resulted in the emergence of world-class companies like Google, amazon, apple, etc, that have been able to satisfy the growing demand of technology, which has surely lacked in various other countries around the world, explaining the difference in GDP.

Growth is very important because it's linked to improvements in living standards. When the economy grows, companies often profit more, potentially leading to higher wages and more job opportunities. Governments also collect more in taxes without raising rates, which can be spent on public services like schools, hospitals, and transportation.

The Real-life Impacts of Economic Expansion and Contraction

Expansion: When the economy is growing, you'll likely see new businesses popping up, more job postings, and generally more optimism about the future. For individuals, this might mean more opportunities for employment and higher incomes, making it easier to afford homes, vacations, or education. For society, economic expansion can fund better public services, reduce poverty, and improve overall quality of life.

Contraction: Conversely, when the economy contracts, it can feel like a harsh winter has settled in. Businesses might freeze hiring or lay off worker, people might spend less out of fear of losing their jobs, and governments might cut spending to balance budgets. This can lead to a cycle of negative effects, as reduced spending leads to lower demand, which in turn leads to more layoffs and even less spending.

Economic contractions can be particularly challenging. **Unemployment rates** can rise, making it difficult for people to find work. Families might need to cut back on spending, delaying major purchases or scaling down their lifestyles. Governments might increase taxes or reduce public services to manage **budget deficits,** further straining household budgets.

Cyclical Nature of the Economy

The economy is inherently cyclical, characterized by periods of expansion and contraction. These cycles are natural, though governments and central banks try to reduce the extremes through policies and interventions. Understanding these cycles helps us prepare for the ups and downs, ensuring we're better equipped to navigate economic changes.

The **GDP** is more than just a number; it is a reflection of our collective efforts, innovations, and challenges. It tells the story of our economy's health and our progress as a society. While not without its limitations—**GDP** doesn't capture everything, like the distribution of wealth or environmental degradation—it's necessary for understanding where we are and where we're heading economically.

CHAPTER 4

THE BALANCING ACT: INFLATION AND DEFLATION

Inflation and **deflation** play starring roles the economics. Understanding these concepts is like learning your ABC's — they tell us the basics of how the value of money changes over time, affecting everything from the cost of a loaf of bread to the stability of nations.

What is Inflation? What is Deflation?

Inflation is when prices rise across the board, reducing the purchasing power of your money. Imagine you can buy a candy bar for $1 today, but next year, due to **inflation**, the same candy bar costs $1.10. You need more money to buy the same thing. **Inflation** at a moderate rate is normal and even seen as a sign of a healthy economy. However, too much **inflation** can be problematic, eroding savings and fixed income's value.

Deflation, on the other hand, is the decrease in the general price level of goods and services. It sounds like a good thing at first—who wouldn't want lower prices? But **deflation** can be a sign of a weakening economy. When prices drop, people might delay purchases, hoping for even lower prices, which can slow economic activity, lead to layoffs, and hurt growth.

Causes and Effects of Inflation and Deflation

Causes of **Inflation** include:

- Demand-pull **inflation**: When demand for goods and services exceeds supply, prices go up.

- Cost-push **inflation**: When the cost of production increases (like a rise in wages or raw materials prices), businesses often pass these costs to consumers in the form of higher prices.

- Monetary **inflation**: When there's too much money circulating in the economy, which can happen if a central bank prints money excessively.

The effects of **Inflation** can be both positive and negative. On the one hand, moderate **inflation** can encourage spending and investment, driving economic growth. On the other hand, high **inflation** can erode savings, increase costs for businesses, and lead to uncertainty in the economy.

Causes of **Deflation** include:

- Reduction in aggregate demand: When consumers and businesses cut back on spending, demand decreases, and prices drop.

- Increase in supply: Technological advancements or improvements in productivity can lower production costs, leading to lower prices.

- Tightening of money supply: When central banks reduce the money supply or raise **interest rates**, it can lead to **deflation**.

Effects of **Deflation** are often negative, including reduced consumer spending, increased debt burden (as the real value of debt increases), and potential economic stagnation or recession.

How Governments Respond to Inflation

Governments and central banks have several tools at their disposal to combat **inflation**:

- Monetary Policy Adjustments: Central banks can increase **interest rates**, making borrowing more expensive and saving more attractive. This can help reduce spending and slow **inflation**.

- **Fiscal** Policy Measures: Governments can reduce public spending or increase taxes to cool down an overheated economy.

- Supply-Side Policies: Improving efficiency and productivity can help increase supply, which can help stabilize prices.

Addressing **inflation** is a delicate balancing act. Raising **interest rates** too quickly can slow economic growth, while not acting can lead to runaway **inflation**. Policymakers must carefully monitor economic indicators and trends to make informed decisions that steer the economy toward stable growth.

Inflation and **deflation** are like the ebb and flow of the economic tide. They are natural parts of the economic cycle, but understanding their causes, effects, and the ways governments respond to them can help us understand the world of personal and national finance.

CHAPTER 5

THE GOVERNMENT'S WALLET: FISCAL POLICY

Fiscal policy is just like the engine of a car, allowing governments to drive the economy toward desired outcomes. Here we will look at **fiscal policy**, exploring how government spending and taxes influence economic activity, as well as delving into the nuances of **budget deficits** and national debt.

Understanding Government Spending and Taxes

Government Spending encompasses all the money spent by government departments and agencies on various services and investments. This can include everything from salaries for public servants to infrastructure projects like roads and schools, to social programs such as healthcare and social security. Government spending injects money into the economy, potentially boosting economic activity and employment.

For example, during the 2008 financial crisis, the U.S. government increased its spending through a stimulus package. This included money for building projects, like roads and bridges, and for programs to help people get jobs.

Taxes, on the other hand, are how the government collects money from individuals and businesses. Taxes can take many forms, including income taxes, sales taxes, and corporate taxes. While necessary for funding government activities, taxes also remove money from the economy. **Fiscal policy** aims to balance these two forces to achieve economic objectives.

The Budget Deficit and National Debt

A **budget deficit** occurs when a government spends more money than it collects in taxes in a given year. To cover this shortfall, governments must borrow money, leading to an accumulation of national debt —the total amount owed by a government to its creditors. While deficits can stimulate economic growth during downturns by increasing spending, sustained deficits and a high national debt can have several implications, including higher **interest rates** and reduced investment in the economy.

Fiscal Policy Tools and Their Impact on the Economy

Governments have two main tools in their **fiscal policy** toolkit:

- Adjusting Government Spending: Increasing government spending can stimulate economic growth by creating jobs and increasing demand. For instance, investing in infrastructure projects not only provides immediate jobs but also improves the economy's long-term efficiency. Conversely, reducing government spending can help cool down an overheated economy but may also slow economic growth.

- Modifying Taxation Levels: Reducing taxes puts more money into the hands of consumers and businesses, encouraging spending and investment. This can be particularly effective in stimulating economic activity during **recessions**. Increasing taxes can have the opposite effect, potentially slowing economic activity but can be useful for controlling **inflation** and reducing **budget deficits.**

The Impact of **Fiscal Policy** on the economy can be significant. Effective fiscal policy can help smooth out economic cycles, reducing the impacts of **recessions.** However, the timing and scale of **fiscal** interventions are extremely important. Missteps can lead to **inflation**, increased debt without stimulating growth, or inadvertently deepening economic downturns.

Fiscal policy also interacts with **monetary policy** (controlled by central banks), and the two must be coordinated for effective economic management. While **fiscal policy** deals with government spending and taxation, **monetary policy** involves managing the nation's money supply and **interest rates**. Together, they form the backbone of a government's economic strategy.

CHAPTER 6

THE CENTRAL BANK'S TOOLKIT: MONETARY POLICY

If fiscal policy pushes the economy forward like the engine of a car, then monetary policy steers it, helping it handle ups and downs. Central banks use tools like interest rates and controlling how much money is out there to keep the economy stable.

The Role of Central Banks

Central banks serve as the financial system's backbone, with responsibilities that include managing the nation's currency, controlling **inflation**, and working to achieve full employment. These institutions, such as the Federal Reserve in the United States or the European Central Bank in the Eurozone, operate with a degree of independence from government to ensure their decisions are made based on economic, rather than political, considerations. One of the primary goals of central banks is to maintain price stability—keeping **inflation** at a moderate, predictable level. Stable prices give confidence among consumers and businesses, which is essential for a healthy economy. Central banks also protect the banking system's health and offer support during financial crises.

Interest Rates and the Money Supply

At the heart of **monetary policy** are two main things: **interest rates** and the money supply.

- **Interest Rates**: Central banks influence the economy by setting the **interest rates** at which banks can borrow money from them (often referred to as the "base rate" or "benchmark rate"). Lowering these makes borrowing cheaper, encouraging businesses to invest and consumers to spend, which can stimulate economic growth. Raising **interest rates** does the opposite, cooling down an overheated economy (where people exchange money too rapidly) and controlling **inflation**.

- Money Supply: This refers to the total amount of money circulating in an economy, including cash and deposits. Central banks can adjust the money supply by buying or selling government securities, influencing **interest rates**, and controlling how much money banks can lend. Expanding the money supply lowers **interest rates** and stimulates economic activity, while contracting the money supply has the opposite effect.

Quantitative Easing and Its Effects

Quantitative easing (QE) is a non-traditional **monetary policy** tool used by central banks to encourage the economy when standard measures (like lowering **interest rates**) have become ineffective, often because rates are already near zero. Through QE, a central bank purchases government securities and other financial assets from the market to increase the money supply and lower **interest rates**, aiming to encourage borrowing, investment, and spending.

The effects of QE can be significant. By injecting liquidity into the financial system, it can help stabilize banks and financial markets in times of crisis, supporting economic growth. However, QE also carries risks, such as potential long-term **inflation** if the money supply expands too quickly, and the devaluation of the currency. Also, by increasing asset prices, QE can contribute to wealth inequality, as those who own financial assets benefit the most.

Through the careful adjustment of **interest rates**, management of the money supply, and, when necessary, the deployment of **quantitative easing**, central banks strive to maintain economic balance.

CHAPTER 7

<u>INTERNATIONAL TRADE AND ECONOMICS</u>

In today's connected world, countries are economically linked. Products, services, and money move across borders, all influenced by the rules of international trade and economics. This chapter looks at the basics of trading between countries, how exchange rates and payments between countries work, and how big world events can really affect local places, showing how everything is connected.

Basics of International Trade

International trade involves the exchange of goods and services between countries. It's driven by comparative advantage, a principle that suggests countries should produce and export goods in which they have a lower opportunity cost compared to others, and import goods in which they are less efficient. This exchange benefits all parties involved, allowing for a more efficient allocation of resources, increased productivity, and access to a wider variety of goods and services for consumers.

However, international trade is also subject to various policies and regulations, including tariffs (taxes on imports), quotas (limits on the amount of a good that can be imported), and trade agreements that aim to reduce barriers and foster trade between member countries.

Exchange Rates and Balance of Payments

Exchange Rates are the rates at which one currency can be exchanged for another. They play a big role in international trade by affecting the price of importing and exporting goods and services. A stronger currency makes imports cheaper and exports more expensive, while a weaker currency does the opposite, potentially boosting a country's export competitiveness.

The **Balance of Payments** is a comprehensive record of all economic transactions between the residents of a country and the rest of the world. It's divided into three main accounts:

- The Current Account includes trade in goods and services, plus earnings on investments.

- The Capital Account records transfers of capital, such as the purchase and sale of real estate.

- The Financial Account captures investments flowing in and out of the country, including stocks, bonds, and government debt.

A **balance of payments** surplus indicates a country is exporting more than it is importing, while a deficit suggests the opposite.

How Global Events Affect Local Economies

The global economy is a network of interdependent nations, where events in one corner of the world can ripple through to others. Here are a few ways global events can impact local economies:

- Trade Disputes: Tariffs and trade wars can lead to increased costs for consumers and businesses, affecting global supply chains and economic growth.

- Financial Crises: Economic turmoil in one country can quickly spread to others through financial markets, leading to widespread economic downturns.

- **Commodity** Price Fluctuations: Changes in the prices of **commodities**, such as oil, can have significant impacts on economies, particularly those that are heavily dependent on exporting or importing these goods.

- Geopolitical Events: Political instability, conflicts, or policy changes in one nation can affect investor confidence and economic activities globally.

CHAPTER 8

ECONOMIC CYCLES AND INDICATORS

The economy is a living, breathing being, constantly moving through cycles of growth and contraction. Like the seasons, these cycles are natural, predictable to some extent, and impact everyone living within the economy.

Identifying Economic Cycles: Growth, Peak, Recession, and Recovery

Economic cycles, also known as business cycles, consist of four main phases:

- **Growth (Expansion):** This phase is characterized by increasing economic activity. Businesses grow, **unemployment rates** fall, and consumer spending increases. It's a period of optimism and investment, leading to a rise in production to meet growing demand.

- Peak: The peak marks the height of economic growth, where the economy operates at maximum output. It's a turning point where growth reaches its limit, **inflation** pressures might rise, and central banks may consider tightening **monetary policy** to prevent overheating.

- Recession: A recession is a significant decline in economic activity spread across the economy, lasting more than a few months. It's visible in industrial production, employment, real income, and wholesale-retail trade. During this phase, businesses contract, unemployment rises, and consumer spending decreases.

- Recovery: Recovery follows a recession, a period where the economy begins to grow again, moving from its lowest point towards a new period of expansion. It's a time of rebuilding and cautious optimism as employment starts to rise, production increases, and consumer spending begins to recover.

Leading, Lagging, and Coincident Indicators

To navigate the economic landscape, economists and policymakers use a variety of indicators:

- Leading Indicators predict the future movements of the economy. They change before the economy as a whole changes, offering insight into the direction in which the economy is headed. Examples include stock market returns, the index of consumer expectations, building permits, and new orders for capital goods.

- Lagging Indicators change after the economy as a whole does. They provide confirmation of the patterns indicated by the leading indicators but aren't useful for prediction. Examples include the **unemployment rate,** corporate profits, and labor cost per unit of output.

- Coincident Indicators change at the same time as the whole economy, providing information about the current state of the economy. These include **GDP**, retail sales, and the unemployment rate.

The Impact of Economic Cycles on Society

Economic cycles have a profound impact on society, affecting everything from individual job prospects to the health of national governments:

- Employment and Incomes: During expansions, employment rises, and wages often increase as businesses compete for workers. During **recessions**, the opposite occurs, leading to higher unemployment and wage stagnation or reduction.

- Public Services: Government revenues, primarily from taxes, fluctuate with the economy, affecting the ability to fund public services. During growth phases, higher revenues can lead to expanded services, while **recessions** can force cuts to these same services.

- Mental and Physical Health: Economic downturns are associated with increased stress, anxiety, and depression, as well as physical health effects due to reduced access to healthcare and healthy food.

- Social Cohesion: Prolonged economic difficulties can strain social bonds, leading to increased social unrest and challenges to political stability.

Understanding economic cycles is like sailing; we can't control the wind, but knowing the signs helps us navigate better.

CHAPTER 9

MACROECONOMICS IN ACTION

Rather than just learning key words and theory, it's always good to look at case studies to see what you have just learnt actually in action.

Historical Economic Events and Their Lessons

The Great Depression (1929-1939): The most profound economic downturn of the 20th century began with the stock market crash of 1929, leading to a decade-long period of high unemployment, falling prices, and severe poverty.

Lesson: It highlighted the need for government intervention in the economy, leading to the development of macroeconomic policies aimed at preventing such deep **recessions**.

The OPEC Oil Embargo (1973-1974): When the Organization of Petroleum Exporting Countries (OPEC) declared an oil embargo against the United States and other nations, it resulted in skyrocketing oil prices and severe economic shocks worldwide.

Lesson: This event showed the vulnerabilities of global economies to energy supply disruptions and the importance of diversifying energy sources.

The Asian Financial Crisis (1997-1998): This crisis was triggered by the collapse of the Thai baht, after the government was forced to float the currency due to lack of foreign currency to support its fixed **exchange rate**, leading to a financial contagion throughout Asia. Countries like Indonesia, South Korea, and Thailand were hit hard, with massive devaluations of currencies, stock market declines, and skyrocketing debt.

Lesson: The crisis showed the dangers of excessive borrowing in foreign currencies and the need for robust financial oversight. It led to reforms in financial regulation and the development of more flexible **exchange rate** systems in many of the affected countries.

The Global Financial Crisis (2007-2008): Originating in the United States with the collapse of the housing market bubble, this crisis quickly spread globally, leading to significant declines in asset values, the collapse of major financial institutions, and a severe downturn in economic activity worldwide.

Lesson: The crisis highlighted the interconnectedness of the global financial system and the risks posed by complex financial products and excessive leverage. It prompted a reevaluation of financial regulation, including measures to increase the transparency of financial transactions and strengthen the capital reserves of banks.

Recent Economic Trends and Their Implications

The Rise of Digital Economies: The last two decades have seen an explosion in the digital economy, characterized by the growth of e-commerce, digital finance, and remote work. This shift has implications for job markets, privacy, and global commerce, emphasizing the need for updated regulatory frameworks and digital infrastructure.

Globalization and Trade Tensions: Recent years have witnessed a backlash against globalization, marked by trade tensions and a reevaluation of free trade agreements. The economic impacts of these shifts show the delicate balance between protecting domestic industries and fostering global trade relations.

Sustainability and Green Economy Initiatives: The growing awareness of climate change and environmental degradation has spurred a global push towards sustainability and the development of green economies. This movement is characterized by investments in renewable energy, sustainable agriculture, and green technologies, aiming to decouple economic growth from environmental harm. The trend towards sustainability has significant implications for energy markets, manufacturing processes, and labor markets, with a shift in job opportunities towards sectors involved in creating and maintaining sustainable infrastructure and technologies. It shows the urgent need for economies to adapt to and mitigate climate change's impacts while presenting new opportunities for innovation and economic development in line with environmental sustainability.

Predictions for the Future of Global Economies

Increased Automation and Artificial Intelligence: The continued advancement of AI and automation technologies is expected to significantly impact labor markets, productivity, and income distribution. Economies may need to adapt to these changes by investing in education and training for jobs of the future.

Climate Change and Economic Policies: As the effects of climate change become more pronounced, economies around the world will increasingly need to integrate environmental sustainability into their growth strategies. This could involve innovations in green technology, carbon pricing mechanisms, and policies aimed at reducing dependence on fossil fuels.

Global Economic Power Shifts: Emerging markets are predicted to play an increasingly dominant role in the global economy, challenging the economic dominance of current superpowers. This shift could lead to a more multipolar world economy, with implications for international trade, investment flows, and economic policy.

Macroeconomics is vast and varied, with lessons of the past, the realities of the present, and the predictions for the future. Historical events remind us of the resilience and vulnerability of economies, while recent trends highlight the ongoing evolution of economic structures in response to technological and geopolitical shifts. Looking ahead, the predictions for global economies call for adaptability, foresight, and a commitment to sustainability.

WHAT NOW?

Congratulations! You've started on a journey through the world of macroeconomics, unraveling the mysteries of economic cycles, **fiscal policies**, and global market trends. But as we reach the end of this book, you might wonder, "What now? How can I apply what I've learned and continue exploring?"

Keep Observing

The world around you is a live laboratory for macroeconomic principles. Watch the news, follow the markets, and observe the economic indicators discussed in this book. How do they reflect the theories you've learned? Can you identify the signs of economic growth or recession in your country?

Go Deeper

This book has laid the groundwork, but there's so much more to learn. Consider delving into related subjects like microeconomics, which focuses on individual and business-level economic decisions, or international economics, which looks at how countries interact financially.

Connect the Dots

Try to connect the economic concepts you've learned with other areas of study, such as history, politics, and environmental science. Understanding how economics intersects with these fields can offer you a more comprehensive view of how the world works.

Engage in Discussions

Share your newfound knowledge with friends, family, or online communities. Discussing economic issues and trends can deepen your understanding and offer new perspectives. Plus, it's a great way to keep the information fresh in your mind.

Think Critically

Question and critically evaluate the economic information you come across. Not all analyses or predictions turn out to be correct, and part of being economically literate is learning to discern between well-supported arguments and mere speculation.

Practical Applications

Consider how the principles of economics can apply to your personal life. Whether it's budgeting your allowance, understanding the impact of **inflation** on your savings, or considering the economics of environmental choices, there are endless ways to make economics a part of your everyday decision-making.

Look to the Future

The world of economics is ever-evolving, with new theories, technologies, and challenges emerging all the time. Stay curious and open to learning. What will be the next big economic trend or challenge, and how will you, as a future leader, economist, or informed citizen, be part of the solution?

Your journey through macroeconomics doesn't end here. It's just beginning. With the knowledge from this book, you're now better equipped to navigate the complex economic landscape of our world. Keep learning, stay curious, and remember—the future of the economy is not just shaped by global leaders and economists but by informed individuals like you.

GLOSSARY

Balance of Payments: A record of all transactions made between one particular country and all other countries during a specified period. It shows the total money coming in and going out.

Budget Deficit: A budget deficit occurs when a government's spending exceeds its revenue.

Commodity: A substance or product that can be traded, bought, or sold

Cyclical: This refers to events or processes that happen in a pattern or cycle, often used to describe the ups and downs in the economy over time.

Deflation: When the general price level of goods and services decreases over time, meaning your money can buy more than it used to.

Exchange Rate: The price of one country's currency in terms of another's. It determines how much foreign currency you get for each unit of your own currency.

Fiscal: Related to government finances, especially regarding spending and revenue collection (taxes). **48**

Fiscal Policy: The government's use of spending and taxation to influence the economy. For example, lowering taxes or increasing government spending to boost the economy.

GDP (Gross Domestic Product): The total value of all goods and services produced in a country in a year. It's like a scorecard showing how well the economy is doing.

Inflation: The rate at which the general level of prices for goods and services is rising, and, consequently, the purchasing power of currency is falling.

Interest Rates: The cost of borrowing money or the reward for saving. High rates can slow borrowing and spending, while low rates can encourage them.

Monetary: Relating to money or currency, especially regarding the total amount of money in circulation or in a country's economy.

Monetary Policy: How the central bank controls the supply of money in the economy, often by changing interest rates to keep inflation in check and the economy growing at a healthy rate.

Quantitative Easing: A monetary policy used by central banks to inject money into the economy to stimulate growth, usually by buying government securities.

Recessions: Periods when the economy is shrinking, not growing. Signs include increased unemployment, decreased spending, and lower production.

Stimulus Package: A set of government spending initiatives and tax cuts designed to boost the economy. It's like a financial push to help the economy grow stronger, especially during times when things are tough, like a recession. The goal is to increase spending and create jobs so that the economy can recover faster.

Unemployment Rate: The percentage of the labor force that is jobless and actively looking for work. It's a key indicator of the job market's health.